Messages

Danielle Glenn

Messages

Copyright © 2016 by Danielle Glenn

PO Box 5881 West Memphis, AR 72303 All Rights Reserved. Except as permitted under the U.S. copyright Act of 1976, no part of this publication may be reproduced, distributed, or transmitted in any form or by any means, or stored in a database or retrieval system, without the prior written permission of the publisher.

ISBN: 978-0-578-17834-9

Dedication

I dedicate this book to my first-born son David Glenn, III. When I gave birth to you, it unlocked something greater inside of me that made me want to go even harder after my purpose. Mommy loves you so much! This book is also dedicated to my family, friends, and Kingdom Seekers International Ministry of Arts church family. I love all of you so much!

Acknowledgments

Wow, this has been an awesome journey. I thank God Almighty for embedding the gift of writing and poetry inside of me to be used for His glory. I thank my parents, Benjamin and Angela Davis, for being supportive of me and giving me life. I also would like to thank my spiritual parents, Jonathan and Jessica Davis, for birthing this gift out of me and for being such a great support to me. Thanks for pushing me to another level. Last, but definitely not least, I give thanks to my husband, David Glenn, Jr., for being an awesome man of God and being supportive in my corner. Thank you for never giving up on me and my gift and always being there when I needed you. I love you so much Babe!

Table of Contents

Dedication

Acknowledgments

DELIVERANCE FROM HURT   4
Damaged Identity
Victor of the Past
Eulogy to Flesh
Deadly Silence

MESSAGES OF HOPE   16
Turn Around
I'm A Survivor
Mirror Mirror
Pineapple Faith
Wilderness of Singleness

SEEDS OF LOVE   33
I Love You
I'm Gone Love or Die Trying
The "L" Word
Mother's Day

RESTORATION IN MARRIAGE   45
Soulmates
For Better or Worse
When a Woman Prays

MY PASSION, MY PURSUIT & MY PURPOSE   54
The Process
Beware of Distractions
God's Backing Me
The Ultimate Fight

SURRENDERANCE & SALVATION   **67**
What Do I Do When I Love God, but I Love Sex, Too?
Can You Hear Me Now?
Lord, Have Your Way
The Plan of Salvation
Celebration of Freedom

REFERENCES   **84**

Messages

DELIVERANCE FROM HURT

Damaged Identity

I was always told that you should have your own identity, be the best you no matter what others may think

As Christians we've given up living righteous and became complacent with living right-ish

Our identities have been wrapped up in our own conscience thinking, comfortable with our flesh instead of seeking God to be delivered out of our mess

Yes, playing hide and go get it with the enemy, being disobedient, believing you was gone get the trophy, trying to take the place of someone else's anointing, hoodwinked and tricked the enemy had you thinking you were the best, but now your identity has been labeled just like the rest

It's a fight everyday between your spirit and flesh. But God is saying, "I'm sick of hearing that same ol' song, I surrender all, but you have become the hindrance of your surrendering"

You can't accept the fact that it's possible to keep your hormones intact, FORNICATION DAMAGED, chains of bondage playing havoc with a spiritual body
You're supposed to be a bad chick, but the only man you try and trap are those who already have an attachment, ADULTERY DAMAGED

You are creative and gifted at what you do, but all you see is money and want to clown when a crowd is around instead of allowing your gift to make room for you, GREED DAMAGED

What I love about damages is that they can be repaired, whatever you have done to someone or whatever someone has done to you, RESTORATION, DELIVERANCE, HEALING, AND FORGIVENESS can take place as long as there's no fear

God is the ultimate craftsman, so allow him to remake and remold you becoming a new creature in him, you will be made over and your identity restored

> *Dear God, I ask that you give your people a clean and fresh start. Cleanse them from all hurt that they may have experienced in their life whether it was something that was done to them or something that they may have done to someone else. Restore every part of their identity in Jesus' name I pray AMEN.*

Victor of the Past

Past
Everybody knows who I am, I'm that thing that has haunted you for years. And fear is the root of it, exposure is just a part of it, some say that I'm good others label me as bad, but hey they just mad because I'm their past. You see I tend to hurt people and leave them captive, strung out, bound by my venom and if you're not careful, you'll be my next victim

Present
Victim, something I never thought I would become, I was promised that as I got older my past would drift away from me further, but yet closer am I drawn with an even tighter bond. Unable to shake loose hearing the rattling sounds of these chains weighing me down to the point to where I can't get up. So I disguise the confused frown turned upside down with a smile so bright, growing up having every tangible thing I ever wanted, but no one even knew though what was hidden past

Past
Hurts and pains is what I use to keep you tangled and bound, even make you feel like you got to deal with it so that you cover how you really feel with a disguise. Your mind is the key to making all this a success and I won't rest cause now you feel like it's your fault, you feel like the rape wasn't real, the verbal and physical abuse wasn't real, I'm forever you and it's my job to make sure you live with this hurt for the rest of your life

Present

Life turned around at the tender age of 10, a hidden secret that would supersede and form an un-natural being growing up being taught that blood is thicker than water, never thought that the same blood would take something so precious given by the father. In my head no one would ever understand, now I am a play writer piecing together scenes to make my future brighter unaware being cast as an actor my past was given a movie deal and is my scriptwriter

Past

Controlling every part of you, the director of your destiny, you have no one so who can you turn to?

Present

The bible says that we overcome by the words of our testimony trying to believe this with thoughts consumed with pure evidence, I need some type of release, something to give this pain relief. The more I cut through my flesh the pain doesn't go away, but only grows deeper at its best maybe I should just put my soul to rest

Past

You think?

Present

I guess, what am I to do this chain is becoming complex, twisted and tangled in its metal knots I want this pain to stop

Past

Yeah right, my job is to keep you bound with constant sleepless nights

Present

Enough, I can't take it no more, to my past I could no longer be employed, chains of bondage, twisted mindset, a hidden agenda from the enemy that made me believe my past was harmless. No longer bound, God I understand now, I cannot be a puppet entertaining the enemy's crowd, no more strings attached breaking every chain no longer riding the bench, but I'm placed on the court as the star in this game.

I realized I am not the victim, but the victor screams coming out of my belly louder than a lions roar, receiving the outpour no more inevitable spills of invisible thrills sending chills to my soul. I'm climbing over walls turning my stumbling blocks into stepping stones, I'm the next Ezekiel so arise these dry bones covered by the spirit of the Lord is the only thing it needs.

So I bury my past in the coffin and become the living dead around here spiritually walking, FREELY VICTORIOUS, I am an overcomer, freedom looks good on me, but God gets all of the Glory, you could be this too if you only break the chains connected to you.

Dear God, I pray that you deliver your people from the past hurts and pains that they are still holding on to. Show them that they are victorious over anything that they may have gone through. I declare that they are a new person in Jesus' name I pray AMEN.

Eulogy to Flesh

Ladies and Gentlemen, we are gathered here today to lay to rest a very old friend of mine and someone who was close to us all

My task is that of a difficult one to most, but I must be honest don't take it the wrong way I'm not here to be boast, just to give the eulogy of someone we all knew most

FLESH was something else with itself going over and beyond to the deeper depths just to bring glory to oneself, selfish

But you see we became best friends, like most of y'all unaware that it was all a scam plotted up by the enemy that we remain besties to the end so I hung with flesh daily walking hand in hand

Flesh was always by my side we practically grew up together, there wasn't nothing we wouldn't do for each other

Somebody come at me the wrong way flesh was the first person to have something to say, never had to turn the other cheek because when flesh would speak it would only be a four letter word technique that would draw more heat, which would leave the other person bruised and beaten, quick to put them hands in your life so don't get caught slipping

Flesh was in defense mode everywhere she would go, but she felt that she had an image to uphold I would try and calm her down because her daddy got sick and tired of hearing about the Pastor's child clowning around town, but I knew the secret

One seed planted at the age of ten, caused flesh to play with its leaves for a number of years

Hiding behind a basketball and jersey flesh told me that skirts were never really for me so I listened because we were best friends we went through the same thing and she didn't want me to get the wrong attention again

Thinking flesh knew my heart so I couldn't counteract so I allowed my gender to do a flip like that

Disguising the woman in me at its best sports bra over breast wife-beater over chest white-T over rest taking the advice of flesh, "yeah you a girl, but who said you had to wear a dress?"

Flesh was real good to me free will, no conscience, no conviction able to do whatever with no restriction our relationship became my addiction

Un-forgiveness linked to anger linked to hatred linked to mind battles linked to suicidal thoughts

I was hoodwinked tricked and deceived by flesh that made me believe my life was really not that big of a mess

A friendship that was never honest and pure so I committed murder to flesh for lying about the pain I endured

No longer content with being a victim but the victor no need to mourn because every day new Grace and Mercies are born

Today is the day we as a family in this gathering, you say to God, "I understand now your will not mine I can no longer be a puppet entertaining the enemies crowd"

Some of you right now understand what I'm saying because at this moment flesh is causing friction with your spirit and you really don't want to hear this

You'd rather go to the bathroom and wait for the benediction but I'm only here to speak truth not give jurisdiction because in the heavenly court system only he rules so be careful because you don't know the day He may be recording you

It's not worth it listening to flesh say, "you don't have to really live righteous just right-ish,"

For if ye live after the flesh ye shall die, but if ye through the spirit do mortify the deeds of the body, ye shall live,

Flesh know the word, but can't stand the conviction in Romans, so it misuses the comfort given in Psalms,

An almost Christian looks right, but lives wrong Something's we have been battling with for way to long and its nobody's fault but our own because we are the hindrance that's keeping our spirits from moving on

So I dare you to bury your flesh in the coffin, connected yet separately become a modern day zombie dead yet living, spirit breathing heavy God's voice speaking clearly take heed to the flesh and give it its own EULOGY.

Dear God, I pray in the name of Jesus that your people will read this and immediately get a hunger to deny their flesh. I plead the blood of Jesus over their minds and declare that they will be renewed. I ask that you show them that they must feed their spirit with more your word, so that they can resist the desires of their flesh. In Jesus' name I pray AMEN.

Deadly Silence

I'm a prisoner of words unsaid
Crazy, fair and unfair thoughts run through my head
I should start to speak, but I stop and keep silent
This is like solitary confinement
My tongue is caged and I dare not fight it
Afraid of what others might say
I should start to speak, but instead I sshhh!!! Keep silent
This silence is killing me, I almost don't have nothing left
Scrapping the earth for a piece of myself
Instead of looking to the one for peace within myself
I'm pregnant with a word in my belly
Lord, help me understand it
My mouth is on lock down and religious traditions plus more has it bound
I dare not have another miscarriage or abortion
Listening to others
And how their word is most important
I bow my head and clinch my stomach
Out of my eyes flows rivers of tears
Once upon a time in my life this was something so weird
These spiritual contractions are coming
I can't hold it no longer
This silence is deadly and could kill me and what's to be born
No more bowed head
I rise and shout the highest praise
HALLELUJAH, GOD IS GOD

I dare not keep quiet
Because what I got might help break someone else's silence
For way to long we have been misconstrued
So I pull out my trumpet and blow it
On all those who were wrongly taught and are now confused
I speak life
I speak love
I speak peace
I speak joy
I speak rest
I speak confidence
The enemy is mad just wishing
He could drag me back to silence
God has greater for me and in me
To much is given much is required
So silence is buried
No longer will I keep quiet

Dear God, I ask that you break the curse of tradition and silence. Build your people up to have the courage and confidence to SPEAK those things that you will allow them to. Give them the strength to decree and declare those things of the Lord. In Jesus' name I pray AMEN.

MESSAGES OF HOPE

The Year of the Turn Around

I was always told that there's nothing new under the sun, so I allowed myself to be stuck in a world of confusion

Bound by the generational curses of un-forgiveness and bitterness, I opened myself up to the enemy's tricks and became my own hindrance

Listening to others instead of the voice of God who is truly my only critic, but I was disobedient and now I got this conflict between my flesh and spirit but which one is stronger

It was evident that I had lost sight of what was important even though I went to church constant I still felt misplacement

Sick and tired of being sick and tired so I acquired wise counsel and they said I must feed my spirit of meat that will never expire

Then God spoke and said everything you went through wasn't for your demise, but to help push someone else towards my prize

A refined warrior built for my Glory placed in the Kingdoms army so you wonder why I'm wild'n because God spoke and said this is the year of the turn around

A change has taken place in my lifestyle no need for me to continuously act juvenile serving God building up my jewels I got a stockpile awaiting for my crown

What the devil meant for bad God flipped it for my good and now I am called the Royal Priesthood

This is the year of the turnaround obviously so my flesh I deny and His word I apply in my heart apparently, what the world thinks is so contrary hands as work feet in movement so swiftly I'm the new Lebron James off the dribble ain't nobody stopping me

This is the year of the turnaround completely so I'm way past the religious mentality because half the church is sleep and the other half is drowsy wake up saints God is looking for us to walk boldly

The year of the turnaround no time to be wasted looking to be blessed so I allowed my faith to decapitate the naysayers my praise leaving the enemy discombobulated

This is the year of the turnaround so allow me to reintroduce Christ the one who took on flesh and became the ultimate sacrifice the one who blocked every STD, AIDS and HIV because your flesh was so easily enticed turned it around and gave you a wife the one who took your lonely sleepless nights turned it around and gave you peace comfort you with the Holy Spirit and said, "sleep tight"

This turn around got me so juiced the Kool-Aid man come and ask me what kind of sweetener I use I tell him this ain't no minute maid, but I do serve a God who created everything turned around and in less than a minute a man was made

I'm geeked up to the next level operating in every creative flow year of the double double so receive the outpour

This is the year of the turnaround no longer in the wilderness because you're now promise land bound.

> *Dear God, I decree and declare that things are turning around in the lives of your people at this very moment. I pray in the name of Jesus that you do a new work with them and increase the overflow over their lives and wherever they may be. In Jesus name I pray AMEN.*

I'm A Survivor

I remember when I looked over my life and finally realized what was taking place

My mind went blank

Another part of me was dying diving as if it were a septic tank

At first, so confused unable to dissect this issue

Thinking who can I turn to

Listening to friends, family, co-workers, and the doctor for my deliverance

I became my own hindrance

Trying to keep the tears intact,

Not wanting my makeup to run because now my womanhood is threatened

So there must be no lack

Can't be caught slipping, my outer appearance must remain sane,

But behind closed doors I can't stop the tears

From dripping down my face as morning rain

Then I hear a small still voice speak and say,

"You're a Survivor"

Then I'm reminded of the scripture that says,

I am more than a conqueror through Christ Jesus

Then I reflect even deeper and I'm reminded that by His stripes I am healed

No longer bound by fear in an uncomfortable position

You see I was diagnosed with spiritual cancer

Unfruitful things and people in my life, killing me slowly causing me this condition

But by tapping into the Holy Spirit my faith destroys any level of sickness

I cannot allow my pain to become my addiction

So the spiritual radiation brought restoration giving me new revelations

This daily dose of chemo causes me to seek Him more

Not only to fully receive the outpour but to fall in love with God even more

Many situations may have come by surprise

But I understand now that it wasn't for my demise

God has given me beauty for my ashes so I must rise

I was born with wings an eagle walking amongst chickens

No longer living on the outer

But to the inner core my spirit is quicken

Inside and out a beautiful being wrapped up in His love

I sit back rocking the identity of victory

In a battle that has already been won.

Dear God, I thank you for every survivor of any test and trial that have come their way. God I speak to those that are still going through YOU ARE A SURVIVOR. Lord I pray that your people tap into the strength of you and realize that they are more than conquerors through Christ Jesus. I decree and declare that you will survive in Jesus' name I pray AMEN.

MIRROR MIRROR

Mirror, Mirror on the wall,

I know He's the greatest of them all

But why is it I struggle with seeing you and not Him at all

I've gotten so caught up in my reflection

That it caused me to limit my faith to a one level dimension

I began to worry about what others see and what I see

Instead of what the ALL KNOWING EYE see

Mirror, Mirror on the wall

Jehovah-Jireh my provider is what He's been called

Shopping until I drop, living in the moment as it swiftly pass by

But Sunday comes around, and now I sit unable to pay my tithes

I've put my focus on my resource instead of the source and listening to His voice when He says, that faith is the substance of things hoped for

Mirror, Mirror on the wall

God the father, God the Son and God the Holy Spirit

I must have all three of y'all

So Lord forgive me for putting others before you

Going listening and talking to them before consulting you

To your voice I dare not harden my heart

Drama I block it out, family I block them out, friends I block them out

Just to see this glimpse of you no one can compare to what I've got

Mirror, Mirror on the wall

This thing right here has gotten deep

That all of the ungodly has been uprooted out of me

Now when I come around people say that I'm acting strange

I don't act, talk, or walk the same

I have a new mindset and to truly live for God I had to change

I know now that the more I starve my flesh and feed my spirit

I am not bound by the worldly system, which is totally rigid

I understand that I have purpose and it is something so unique

And now since there's a different me

Oh, dear mirror, mirror we no longer need to speak

I've got someone else I can talk to

And only His vision and will

I will seek.

> *Dear God, I pray that you show your people a mirror image of themselves. God show them the areas that they are lacking and the areas that they need to trust you more in. God I pray that your people have a receiving heart of change that you are going to make in them and the change that you are making right now at this moment. In Jesus name I pray AMEN.*

Pineapple Faith

I was given an assignment, she said I need you to speak on faith and compare it to a fruit

We trying to bring health awareness in the spiritual and natural and this is something that you must do

God gave me a Pineapple, which is a covered fruit

He began to download things to me and He said, "now use what I give you"

During an analysis of the pineapple I realized that there might not be something on the inside

But faith without works is dead and I must activate what's already been said

So hard as a pineapples shell, my faith knocks down and rattles the ground and unlocks the jail that Paul and Silas was held

I begin to study and I begin to pray
I found out in Hebrews 11:1 that, "Now faith is the substance of things hoped for and the evidence of things not seen"

So when I speak those things that be not as though they were

I began to break down barriers

I dare not listen to the naysayers
Like blind Bartemaeus, my faith decapitated my haters

Cut up like a pineapple in chunks, wedges and slices

My faith screams out because it just can't keep silent

I sat in a classroom one day and listened to what the instructor had to say

"Go to college, graduate with honors, be all you can be" here it is I'm out of school with a Bachelor's degree and the job market don't seem to fair if you ask me

You see school couldn't teach me that God is not limited to one classification

He is the I am that I am and Webster dictionary couldn't give me that definition

I know that faith is my key which gives me access

Because Ephesians tells me "in whom we have boldness and access with confidence by the faith of Him"

Romans 10:17, "so then faith cometh by hearing and hearing by the word of God

To my faith I applaud, this may seem odd

But we've created a bond

Deeper than the ocean floor it goes way beyond

No nonsense, but concepts

Like the outer core of a pineapple it could be complex

But forsaking all I'll trust Him, so I've been granted access to the Kingdom above

Because He loves me like a strawberry contrary to what others may think

His peace soothes my soul, like a lemon heaven sent dropped in a bag of tea

Gentle as a peach, it's His voice when He speaks to me

Sour with correction, yet sweet as an apple is His goodness towards me

Packing power like a grape, great is His meekness shown

Trials and tribulations come to make me strong

Because longsuffering comes with a covering

And as I wait patiently for the unveiling of the seeds that were planted

More than in a watermelon, my faith is pushed to a deeper dimension

Make a joyful noise loud and tangy like an orange, because from the very beginning that's what we were created for

Stamina curved in a banana I rush with endurance peeled with temperance, I must make a difference because God sent His Son, which was oh so generous

My faith is not swept away with the waves

But has a tropical taste

Like a pineapple at the first glance you get an eye full

And when cut through the juices flow of mercy and grace

Like an anointed pineapple dipped with a super natural glaze

This is my Pineapple Faith.

Dear God, I pray that you increase the faith of your people. Help them to understand that If they are able to put their trust in you and give you their all no matter what comes their way; you will always be there by their side. In Jesus name I pray AMEN.

Wilderness of Singleness

There was a time in my life where I felt lost and didn't know where to turn

I felt as if I was cursed because every relationship I got in never got better but only worse

I learned to disguise my true feelings of being empty so I wore a smile of a lie that accepted anything a piece of a man I thought was missing could be a part of me

Voids needing to be filled, lustful desires my flesh will always appeal to something I couldn't have but it always seem to be in my grasp

An independent woman navigating through the day pay my own bills making My Own Way, needless to say I had a kitty who only like to go out after dark because at this point she would feel a spark to let out a silent meow every time a dog will bark

I thought image was everything and could catch the right man, the way my hips would swing

Yeah he bought me shoes, purses, clothes, and every piece of bling, The way he provided I just knew I'd get the ring, but turns out I was only his plaything, he had already found and crowned his queen

So now I'm dressed up as a bad chick, but sprung on a man who already has an attachment

Desperate now, my own self I had to persuade I'm sick of being everyone's bridesmaid, so I settled for the music industry thinking it was God because he told me that he prayed and heaven sent me

Every beat that was created I thought it would be a reminder of the love we made, but his fist became the sticks, but for a moment I didn't mind I told him all of me was his only because I was promised by this little drummer boy I will always be his rib

Stuck, bound, wanting to get out but I don't know how I became the modern-day little red riding hood lost in this forest until I was giving instructions on how to get through this wilderness

An experience I could not avoid with marriage as my goal I had to be detoxified from every soul tie

Which in God's eye is dissatisfaction, now aware of every distraction

Since my perception has changed I can't allow my spirit to go through the same rotation of being separated from Him because it's not hard it's a choice

In preparation now of being delivered from singleness in the right position to be blessed as his MRS

Emotions contained not running rapid, no longer attracted to the physical appearance but looking to be found in the spirit

Never settling again realizing I was never cursed but blessed, located in the place where God got me, I have his address, he has become my husband giving him total access waiting for my earthly Boaz to manifest

I'm sprung on this guy named Jesus with no strings attached His pureness is Rich from above focused on pleasing him, so I can't allow myself to be drunk in love, can't risk being tipsy because I must maintain stability

My worth is too valuable as I say this quoting the author Jessica Davis, daughter your wilderness experienced is a time of purging from your past to prepare you for your promise, embrace your journey getting through the wilderness of singleness.

Dear God, I pray that you give those that are going through wilderness of singleness experience comfort. Lord show them that this is only a process and teach them how to embrace this place so that they would be able to handle the next place that you take them .Lord allow your people to draw closer to you and you open the door to send them their Esther or Boaz. Strengthen their minds and hearts in Jesus' name I pray AMEN.

SEEDS OF LOVE

I Love You

When a mother says,

"I love you," it comes from a place within her heart reaching back from the very start the pregnancy test read positive

Her love is not contingent on things and what others may think, but it pushes you to a level unknown causing your inner man to speak out loud to do better just to make mother proud

When a father says,

"I love you," he's reminded when the doctor said whether it was a boy or a girl and this unlocked the door of a whole new world

His love caused his instinct to kick in of being a protector and provider, realizing of his family he was the only driver with the grace to take everyone higher

When a brother says,

"I love you," it expresses that he would always have your back

His love is there to pick up the slack, no matter right, wrong or under attack, the bond is tighter than any other

When a sister says,

"I love you," is comes from a sensitive place where her love is easily embraced

It reiterates that of mothers and could never be replaced, secrets shared tucked away in your memory's bookcase

When a husband says,

"I love you," his mind travels back to the day he purchased the ring and got down on one knee just to ask, "Will you marry me?"

Never did he think he would have someone to grow old with, his love matures him for you causing the mistakes made to be that of very few

When a wife says,

"I love you," it triggers that very first phone conversation, smiling from ear to ear, just for you to call and say, "I'm thinking about you," is all she wanted hear

Her love is not boastful, but it bleeds submissiveness, honoring you as her king and not being apprehensive

When a friend says,

"I love you," it's covered with trust, an unshakeable foundation able to bounce back from any situation

Their love does not have an ulterior motive, but it shows growth of receiving and outpouring

The love of all of these sits in their own category, but there is a love known of an even greater story

When God says,

"I love you," it is His word
For God so loved the world that He gave His only begotten Son and Jesus showed His love willfully dying for an ungrateful people

God's love is a promise keeper, after flooding the earth He gave a covenant that can be seen that of a rainbow no matter rain, sun or snow

When God says,

"I love you,"
It carries a great meaning so much that he breathed in you Him, giving you His creativity

His love expresses His grace and mercy constantly giving chances, opening your eyes looking pass religious controversy and seeing the relationship that's needed

God's love is unmatched and irresistible allowing you to read this poem showing to Him your worth and value.

Dear God, I pray that you show your people that you love them even more than those they can physically see. Show them the power in your love and increase the love that they have for each other even the more. In Jesus' name I pray AMEN.

I'm Gone Love or Die Trying

The bible says that love hides a multitude of faults, but why is it that we as Christians have our love locked away in a secret vault

Looking out in the world there is so much confusion and chaos, right in the midst of the enemy's tricks, schemes and plot

Many people have ran, tucked their tail, and hid in a shell not wanting to do ministry because they would be called judgmental missing the reality that there are souls we must pursue

I was once one of those people too, I would talk about what I was going to do or what I wanted to do, but for some reason never get it through

I did what on an average most people would do, I placed myself in a box, but it was more like a cellblock

Arrested by my own nonsense, until I was given a court date dismissed with understanding, realizing Jesus was always there as my defense because for my life he sparred no expense

Now with a renewed mind and a clean heart I'm gone love or die trying supplied with everything I need embracing more patience and longsuffering

Going out into to world just like Jesus walking many roads and streets allowing my light to shine winning souls for the Kingdom so that God be glorified

As I go and minister to that smoker or alcoholic, my love will break through to them being under the influence traveling through their ears and hit their spirit

With God my love reaches out and snatches a woman off the streets, reaches out snatching a fornicating man from having different women in his sheets, no longer bound by sexual perversion covered by His blood they are a new person

Reaching into the school district and casting down the spirit of disrespect and rebellion my love is on a mission

Others may not like to see me coming their way, but I didn't come for the religious crowd, those group of people always at church wearing a frown, those leaders who have misrepresented their position and have hidden behind protocol and tradition, those who look down on a generation who are lost needing to be found

Truthfully they can get the same word because little do they know from God they've also strayed so they might not want to hear what I have to say, but I'm still gone love or die trying anyway

To see someone through the eyes of Christ takes maturity, I'm gone love or die trying knowing that His timing is not my timing I must be about my Father's business I can take the hitting, backbiting, and being lied on because the work of winning souls is tremendous.

Dear God, I pray that you increase the hunger of your people to go reach out to others. I pray that the love of God will shine through them so great that others will come running wanting to be saved. I declare it done in Jesus' name I pray AMEN.

The "L" Word

Since the very creation of time, the "L" word was the very foundation of it all Love

Love had a plan

Created the world in seven days without using its hands

Love breathed life into man and be became a living soul

Gave him work, saw his loneliness so he created him a lady

There are so many times where love can be taken for granted

Things going good in a relationship only when something is given and is called love

It's really lust, those things only satisfying the flesh

Saying one thing to get what you want lies and not love

Lust of the eyes, lust of the flesh and the pride of life

Is how many people misinterpret love

Lost joy in laughter caused others to lose the luxury of living a free life

But knowing Jesus as not only savior, but as
Lord lessons are learned

And Longevity is promised

It's not too late to get an understanding of the "L" word it's not complex

It's just the Lord is love which linked to us gives life.

Dear God, I pray that you show your people the power in Love. Take them back to the very foundation of Love and teach them how to embrace love. In Jesus' name I pray AMEN.

Mother's Day

From day one you have worn many hats

Expressing your love not only through your words, but your actions

Which is a fact we wouldn't be here if your prayers weren't stacked

Up late at night, not willing to throw in the towel of this fight

Raising children of different generations with a spiritual determination to help us to get to know God for ourselves

The most important occasion

On this day we say thank you

Thank you for being a willing vessel created and sculpted by the one and only king

Who took the fragrance of a flower, the majesty of a tree, the gentleness of morning dew, the calm of a quiet sea, the beauty of the twilight hour, the soul of a starry night and the grace of a bird in flight you see, oh my what a masterpiece

Thank you for being patient even when we strayed away and we purposely wanted to disobey

Being disobedient to the fact that all of our actions will have a price to pay, you never left us you were always there midway

Thank you for your encouragement and support

Through all of our ups and downs heartache and tears, you never showed any fear, but everyday your faith appeared

Just like Jeremiah you have that fire shut up in your bones, keeping the family warm, the Holy Spirit comforting you and to us all He reaches out His arms

Thank you for the spiritual birth because now we understand our purpose and worth that our works must be completed on earth

And every gift is to bring God Glory and reach the un-churched so they can receive their birth

Words cannot express how much you mean to us

Your heart is indescribable and your beauty is ageless

Thank you for taking the burns because your ashes produced boldness with a captivating spirit of meekness

The enemy will always be out done because you are more than a Phenomenal Woman, but you rate that of a Proverbs 31

Thank you for not sparring the rod and spoiling the child

Because truth be told if you haven't we all might be somewhere at Charter Lakeside

So we salute you on this day Woman of Grace

With a heart so big reaching inner space

Whether you're a natural mother or a spiritual one

You help bring life to us all with your words of wisdom.

Dear God, I thank you for blessing us all with mothers both natural and spiritual. Thank you for equipping them with the anointing and grace to be able to birth us out. God I pray that you strengthen mothers and send an outpour of your blessings to them. Lord, I ask that you forgive us for taking them for granted, when they saw something in us that we did not see in ourselves. In Jesus' name I pray AMEN.

RESTORATION IN MARRIAGE

Soulmates

Question asked, "will you marry me?" with a response of "yes" so now time to prepare for the gathering

Bridesmaids, groomsman, flower girl, ring bearer, preacher, family, friends, reception, and a party, but understand our passion for each other was predestined way before the setting of the ceremony

A missing link gripped by the hand of God with a seed of passion planted on the inside carrying the anointing of Esther only recognized by the King now released which was once my missing piece joined together are we

Never separated no matter the circumstance able to withstand any task or trial the wait was worthwhile my soulmate our search began even before you and I were a child

The ability to minister and worship with each other however we please, love rolled off the tongue passion leaking to our knees, there is an overflow of love

My cup runs over with thoughts of you loving me as Christ loves the church so powerful making me smile from the inside out

We are mated together, always by your side the foundation of our love is the drive, it shows that I ride for the team because of the goal to win souls and the purpose in the verses that makes our marital status even more virtuous

Yes, true enough we have been through somethings that I will never understand, we've encountered some situations that were never in our game plan

But you as my soulmate makes every bitter moment sweet our love blended together creating only one lung, one love and one heartbeat

Dear God, I thank you for every marriage and I pray that you increase their bond even the more. Show them the purpose of their marriage and why you placed them together. In Jesus name I pray AMEN.

For Better or For Worse

Cloud nine the moment I laid eyes on you our souls connected on a level that I just couldn't pass by reaching beyond the sky your kiss your touch your love has given me an even greater high
You became my purp my dro inhaling that special part of you I'm so throwed, throwed off this love a union destined from above. As I walked down the aisle my heart wears a smile as I think to myself this new step in life has got to be worthwhile

Meanwhile in my head thoughts of us having a child, a son to carry the legacy, I'm ready to login, into this lifestyle

Pictures of you and me together forever God was so generous placing me by your side how clever hand in mine Body pressed against mine able to do whatever whenever

However time has gone by, seconds minutes hours days months years things are not the same if only this clock could rewind then maybe things would change it seems as if our honeymoon was short lived and the dates have been rearranged, cooking cleaning work and school no time for love making in the afternoon I'm sick of giving my all and receiving nothing in return this right here might need to take a pause

Let's see did make the best decision for me? I'm grown I should be able to come and go as I please, I thought this marriage would be a breeze, a slice of Apple pie covered with cherries, looking at other folks they can't be that happy it's all a tease he say he just want to hang with his

boys the single ones who always got something up their sleeves even though one is married
But still is slicker than grease the same one who was slapped with child support by his wife's friend because they had a baby
I thought you were my Adam and I was your Eve I'm about to leave I need some type of relief this marriage has become a tragedy You causing me too much grief

He says this is my fault just like Eve questioning saying, "who you been talking to? Got you contemplating thinking you could lead, you better quit disrespecting me"

But I'm not taking all the blame you see, so he can stop trying to put it all on me because God gave him authority the head of us but he became neck allowing the enemy to distract him with his best I replied my Adam swallow your pride, your steps I was willing to follow but they turned into a glide your back was turned on me thinking if you work a 9-5 my every desire would be supplied seeking for protection I believe I was deceived

Knees barely hitting the floor I can't take it, I'm not doing this anymore

Until God speaks and reminds us both of the covenant that we not only made to each other but to Him God the Father

Now with a clear understanding that our marriage was predestined so
I will fight for you
God forgive us for not seeking wise council and trying to do things our own way that we couldn't handle

We are not my enemies we are now prepared for combat with this comeback I forgave him and he has forgiven me

Heart unthawed once frozen I got the revelation many women were called but I was chosen I dare not have another spiritual abortion unable to birth out you my man of God which is most important I earned my "R" so I know you hearing from God is not bizarre

In his face I must continue to stay so that I would not act like a juvenile fool and mishandle my God given gift which is you, even though our worse got bad our for better produced our greater and now I'm looking to go higher in every area

This is the beginning of something great a new place

I love you so much there's no place I would rather be a union destined to take place even before the foundations of the world
you are the ordained husband
I will stick it out with you keeping God first, no matter what FOR BETTER OR FOR WORSE.

Dear God, I pray that you teach every husband and wife how to take the good with the bad. Teach them how to look pass those natural disagreements and take them back to when they connected in the spirit. I plead the bold of Jesus of every marriage that is ordained in your name. draw them even closer together in Jesus' name I pray AMEN.

When a Woman Prays

Now I lay me down to sleep I pray the Lord my soul to keep and if I die before I wake, I pray the Lord my soul to take

A prayer that was taught in which a foundation was laid As a young girl I was always told to pray, God will hear me it was our conversation

But as I became a woman I had to come to the realization that my prayers had to go beyond my denomination

A single woman quicken to be promiscuous with a spirit of fornication because in my hips I had thicken

Unable to with-hold but truth be told I had Jim, Doug, and Tyrone attached to my soul

Wanting more for myself understanding my worth so I went down on my knees and I prayed,

"God I'm in need of a cleansing both outward and inwardly forgive me for contaminating my temple constantly. I repent and I call back my spirit and return every one of theirs I declare I am free. Give me the strength I need as I enter this quest of singleness as I await for my man of God to manifest. In Jesus name Amen."

A different me, with a heart to please God

I fell in love instantly with keeping His commandments bumped up to another degree

In the spirit is where he found me

Because I had the right positioning my King was on a search for his favor piece

Exactly what I prayed for took place in the spirit and then came to past naturally

A marriage ordained by God, hearts overflowing
The love I have for my husband was insane
Honeymoon short-lived reality kicked in we still had bills

Steady fussing and fighting this relationship became unexciting

A wall now placed between us and I didn't see the handwriting blinded by our own carnal thinking

We lost sight of whom we should first be submissive, headed down a path of destruction until my prayer life received a reintroduction

So I became a modern day Esther, understanding for my marriage, ministry, and family I was the only birther

On my knees I went and begin to pray,

"Lord teach me patience with the ability to speak as a wise woman taming my tongue and building my king with inspiration. Forgive us for not representing our marriage as Christ and the church. Thank you for not letting is go but yet being gracious and merciful. Now I decree and declare that we are on one accord and our marriage is repaired. I'm ready for war as I continue to seek you more blocking out anything and anyone that's a hindrance of receiving your outpour. God I thank you for giving me the endurance that I need and every time I feel myself get weak I speak the wind of God to blown on me."

A great stirring takes place when a woman prays

Anything unlike God cannot stay and everything that needs to come in alignment will rush to its place

When a woman prays her words have the ability to shake the earth

Placed under pressure her diamonds have great worth

Suited up for battle in a zone so swift with her words speaking in an unknown tongue

A woman that prays is a spiritual sniper killing every demon her rolls reversed from a crier to a fighter

When a woman prays it's not for selfish desires or pleasure but with the use of wisdom has the ability to break chains and unlock heavenly treasures

When a woman prays it expresses her strength, love and confidence that she is built to fight and born to win.

Dear God, I pray that you increase the prayer life of every woman and man as well. Teach them the significance in their prayer life. I decree and declare a greater communication with you amongst your people. In Jesus' name I pray AMEN.

MY PASSION, MY PURSUIT, & MY PURPOSE

The Process

I always knew that I was different, you see in my life I've been through many ups and downs

Misguided future with unfruitful seeds planted, thinking I could easily buy my way to heaven

Since I come from a long line, generations of preachers and pastors, but I was never taught no one could serve two masters

I thought I was cool because it was prophesied that I had great gifts in my belly, a word I apparently ignored

I needed a quick trip, so I tried to fast forward my life from the first to the fourth quarter

But nothing seemed to go right, too much wasted time and sleepless nights, I was constantly getting shot down by bringing a knife to a gun fight

I was trying to get to something,

My inheritance

But didn't know in between the prophecy and the promise is

The process

Nevertheless I thought I had already gained much success

Believing I made my own way, which only gave me access to more stress, I really needed to reinvest but my mind was gone because I figured I'm saved and enough God I already possess

Until God spoke and said you will never get to the Promised Land without going through the process

So here I am caught in what I think is a whirlwind

Spinning yet controlled by the father on the tip of His finger
He is the original Harlem Globetrotter

Stripping me of every worldly thing my process was purging every part of me outward and inwardly of everything I had gotten illegally

Because of the false evidence that appeared real I adhered to its tactics

Just like the Children of Israel even though I left Egypt

I still knew how to work with my hands unknowingly suppressed

So I built a golden café because I wanted to payless

Steady going in circles yet shoes never worn out

Until I caught the revelation I was keeping myself bound
You see the process is the best place covered with much grace an area u had to embrace, disobedience to God living

on Earth you just taking up airspace so don't get caught slipping, you will easily be replaced

I thought this process of going through this wilderness experience would be a hindrance to me trying to do me but instead I found myself and now I march with a different army blessed by the one and only Commander in Chief, who calls me His mouthpiece

Who was placed in the streets to bring a word so unique so listen as God speak

God says, "I am the all-knowing and seeing, I need for you to go through this process properly no more disagreeing, I've already given you a glimpse of treasures guaranteed, what's it going to be? The choice is yours, I have opened many doors that will soon close because you have mishandled my outpour, I'll never put more on you than you can bear, so if you feel down or lost I am He who restores. If my will you abide, then thy feet I will guide, every stride will be blessed because you embraced the process where your anointed gift had to expand

My plan has always been for you to make it to the Promised Land, now you have my brand marked by my artistic hand

Go ye therefore with progress fulfilling the process."

Dear God, I pray that your people embrace whatever process that you might be taking them through in their life. Teach them how to go through it successfully so that they won't have to continue to go through the same cycle. In Jesus' name AMEN.

Beware of Distractions

I was never taught that my gift was ministry, so I kept my mouth shut everything inside of me now bound

Afraid that if I brought it forth, others wouldn't really be feeling me

Unaware of the distractions surrounding me, instead of looking to God the one I'm supposed to please I fell into the trap of others and what they need

I begin to realize that a distractions comes from an interaction that you had with someone or something that wasn't fully packing the word that is, and it caused you to have a reaction

So now you so caught up in your flesh, that while it pleases the outer man

It causes you to seek God less and less

The bible tells us that the enemy comes to steal, kill and destroy, so when off focus the enemy can easily shoot and score

It's because our actions caused us to get attracted to the distraction

Now you find yourself in a struggle, listening to others and their opinions instead of going to God the one above you

Coming in many different shapes and sizes

A distraction comes along dragging baggage and all kinds of surprises

Friend, family, neighbor, enemy

Clothes, cars, houses, and material things

Man, woman, boy, or girl,

Out shopping for toys that your child don't even deserve

Night shift, day shift, 9 to 5

Car note, mortgage, rent, cable, gas bill, electric bill, phone bill,

Child support, IRS, house supplies, school supplies

You sit back and think, aw man I forgot to pay my tithes

The Kingdom of God is our occupation

We have the authority to overtake, overcome and over power, because it all comes from our heavenly sponsor

God says, "I know you and you know me and lately things have changed, it seems the definition of our relationship has been rearranged, I need you to walk a little closer to me, come and get back to that place where we used to be"

My brothers and sisters please be alert of the enemy

Beware of the traps that he tries to set before thee

Understand God has never left you always will abide in and stand with you

We are needed in the Kingdom, so beware of distractions

Because it's nothing but a trick of the enemy trying to deceive you.

Dear God, I pray that your people will beware of every distraction that the enemy will send their way. I pray that you open their spiritual eyes to see it and notice it when it comes. I pray that your people will be more alert and have an understanding of having a relationship with you God. I decree and declare that every persons spirit will be awaken right now in the name of Jesus. Thank you for conviction and correction. In Jesus' name I pray AMEN

God's Backing Me

For so long I tried to do things on my own

I figured I would make my own way, do things in my timing since I am grown

But the truth is I really didn't have a plan or a backbone

I was really afraid of succeeding in the things of God so I did what was commonly known

Degrees, careers, money a success in the natural, but a spiritual failure

I was headed in the red zone

Confused and unstable I became a human cyclone

My spirit laid in the graveyard signed with people pleaser on my tombstone, I was one of the unknown

Until one day God spoke to me and said," I have created you so unique, a gift placed inside of you purposely to help bring salvation deliverance restoration and healing to the body use what I've given you"

And that's when I understood that God was backing me

I've been given a new backbone, my flesh and what others think has been overthrown

I'm moving forward going harder after the things of the Lord

God is backing me so I don't mind speaking or decreeing thus said the King

Because His word is never misleading, but correcting and comforting

Gifted with a pen, so as He speaks I write

Words leaping off a page becoming a revelation
for somebody God's word giving them life

I cannot go back, lives and souls are at state

I can't afford to be replaced so I must utilize the wisdom, integrity, loyalty and dignity that the Lord embedded in me and be that Girl gone WILD in these streets

Having nothing to lose because God is backing me.

Dear God, I pray that your people get a true revelation of your grace and mercy. Show them that when they operate in the things that you have ordained for them, you will forever be backing them. Lord, even when they might go astray let them know that you are still there with open arms ready to receive them back. Give your people a push to go harder after you. In Jesus' name I pray AMEN.

The Ultimate Fight

ROUND 1

The bell rings and I look over at my opponent and it seems there is no comparison

I'm a lightweight champion going up against the heavyweight stronghold

As soon as we touch gloves we dance around the ring going toe to toe, he throws the first swing because he got a crowd watching with an image to uphold

We tussle, smashing each other with gloves as enemies in the fight over who is weaker and who has more power

Each punch I take, but I can't quit and become the devoured

Tired, bruised and weak the boxing ring has been turned into WWE wrestling and I began to get tag teamed by lying, hate, lust, rebellion, anger, suicide, depression

Every time I'm hit I fall to the enemies delight, I thought I could use the skills gained from my past and present hurts and pain

But this wasn't a street fight

I try to get dirty, he'll get dirtier, it was like he knew my every move and was my play write

So tired of being knocked out and knocked down so I went to God for a rewrite

ROUND 2

I had a talk with my coach and His team and I was reminded of the strength instilled within me
In the spiritual weight room knowledge and wisdom I consumed

Now as I bob and weave and swiftly move my feet

It's like fire shut up in my bones and now every punch of strongholds is overthrown

Power coming from the almighty God who sits on the throne with the Holy Spirit attached as my backbone

A life as pure as Jesus reaching every time zone

Never thought I had something to prove why should I lose

I'm building up my stamina I've gotten so tired of failing miserably so here I give you my testimony freely

The enemy once had the key to my life and became my locksmith

But now he got to swing even harder with his tactics

Because my faith is so strong with a left hook like Mike Tyson, roles reversed I'm the heavyweight champion, my anointing was God sent

Power packed words speaking, decreeing and declaring those things of the Lord

I'm committing lyrical homicide with a mouthpiece like no other

Knocking out every stronghold leaving them in a coma with the knowledge flowing from my lips call me Mannie Pacquiao from Mexico speaking in a unknown tongue

I'm a lethal weapon a story untold is a must handwritten too much power your pen might bust

ROUND 3

Not ever taking another knockout this match is going down in history as a classic I became the legendary title holder

Fear can't win, mind battles can't win, no stronghold would ever win I'm victorious you can call me Queen of the Ring

I got the victory in every area of my life no longer bound by the slithering sounds of the enemy whispering to me, trying to take me off focus to get a quick hit off me

I'm the winner of this fight leaving the enemy decapitated with his tricks and scams discombobulated no longer are his works being tolerated that's like Sugar Ray Leonard verses Joe Frazier a fight that's way overrated

I'm a part of the new breed with an indescribable identity with a one hitter quitter that is life transforming

I've been given the championship belt call me Ali because Foreman should've known better to step into this ring

I'm bringing the heat with every swing so every imp which is an offspring beware of my sting

A lion without a roar talking a whole lot of noise, the enemy aka the new pretty boy Floyd

I see you stronghold, but I don't feel you

You like a hologram somebody prepare the body bag

I'm pumped up into overdrive going harder climbing over who the world says the best

Steady laying demons to rest stepping into the ring with me the enemy became live bait

I'm killing him and now I just turned this boxing match into the next case on First 48.

Dear God, I pray that your people will be able to fight through any stronghold that might try to keep them bound. I pray that your people will develop a hunger to withstand any battle and take every punch and still stand tall. I decree and declare that their spiritual muscles will develop even greater. In Jesus' name I pray AMEN.

SURRENDERANCE & SALVATION

What Do I Do When I Love God, but I Love Sex, too?

So I once had a problem, an issue that I thought no one could help me solve

No one had a clue, yeah I love God but I love sex, too

It wasn't always like this until I had an encounter with my best friends cousin as he grabbed and gripped me inappropriately I tried to scream,

But when his job was complete he told me he really liked me and not a word of this I could ever speak because I was 10 and he was 17 and much trouble it would be

With tears in my eyes I told him he really hurt me and he said next time it will be easy

So by the time I had turned 13 innocence was gone and curiosity had been unlocked within me

Now as a grown woman I thought my life was set

Good job, house, bills paid with no debt, but honestly my mind was offset

Yeah I went to church, I love God and I know my sins he would forget

Unable to control this piercing feeling my flesh was upset

Because the cold showers couldn't cure my night sweats

In my own thoughts I had only one outlet

I called my guy better known as bae, and I told him what I was going through and he said that he would come over and watch a movie or two I said cool knowing it will lead down another avenue

It wasn't really bad we only had sex occasional and I didn't know what else to do I mean I love God, but I love sex, too

With my guy in my presence not thinking of God's presence

My fleshly kitty let out a meow so intense, spreading eager legs at any expense

Never felt that my bed was defiled since he was the only one in it was my defense

The screams, the moans and then a quiet sigh, no more movement as I laid in his arms feeling like I was protected

But suddenly realizing there was no protection, afraid that the cum inside of me would become something inside of me

I love God so that morning I prayed forgive me I thought he would hear me since I figured I'm still apart of His team

This sexual addiction had me slipping into behaviors you wouldn't believe

Pondering on several nights activities, opened the door to masturbation and pornography

A part of me felt trapped as if I had become spiritually handicapped my life was under attack

So I begin to cry out to God

I need you like never before, I can't do this on my own

Then God spoke and said, "I sent a prophet in the land to help hold you accountable, she will guide you through this wilderness experience of singleness"

As I began to cling to her wings I got a better understanding that during the times of temptation and falling into sexual sin I was not under God's covering, but off doing my own thing

I understand that sex was only being used to numb the pain of broken heartedness

Cries of ecstasy to hide my tears of loneliness this sexual perversion was a seed planted by the devil to cause spiritual abortion

I am stronger than I once was to my surprise

Keeping a clear mind games and tricks I cannot allow

Listening to R&B would easily cause my flesh to arouse and unintentionally end up in someone's sheets and my process I will continue to repeat and never meet the man God has for me

Yeah sex is good, let's not get that misunderstood

I love God enough to stay on a narrow path and not stray away

No longer creating soul-ties as the enemy's playmate my love for sex can wait until the day I marry my mate

There is nothing more to negotiate

I am sold-out to God so I unaffiliated myself with the world and live according to God's word.

Dear God, I pray that your people will be able to withhold from operating in things that are unlike you. I pray that you give them self-control and that you strengthen them. Allow them to get lost in you and their purpose. In Jesus' name I pray AMEN.

Can You Hear Me Now?

John 10:27 says, "My sheep hear my voice and I know them and they follow me." John 8:47 says, "Whoever is of God hears the words of God. The reason why you do not hear them is that you are not of God."

I know that I am nothing without your voice piercing my ears reaching to the depths of my spirit

So many things going on, God help me understand, confused by the things I see with lifted hands, singing in the choir, yet with a pure passion for R&B

Confused by what I see, ministering bible toting gospel preaching, but at home a misguided family, where is the teaching?

Off balanced, killing, people up and dying, sitting around thinking you got time, but your time is not His timing

SSSSHHH!!!! God is speaking

Can you hear me now? I'm calling for an awakening in the body, for too long you have mishandled, mistreated and misrepresented me and the gifts that I have embedded in thee

Wake up you are a part of the king and no, I never said this journey would be a cool-breeze I'm trying to get your attention, but most of the church is sleep and the other half is drowsy

Can you hear me now? My children know my voice and understand the plan of the enemy, his tricks are deceitful and conniving got you playing the lottery when gambling is not of me, so how dare you put every blessing on me

You cannot serve two masters, so you choose where you are trying to live happily ever after

I'm tired of you mistreating this marriage and taking what I give you for granted I've been here too long so I cannot allow this union to be annulled

Can you hear me now? I'm soon to come back riding on a pearly white cloud, looking for my bride without a spot, wrinkle or blemish, no need to try and hide those things which are a hindrance

So uncover girl, I'm seeing right through all of that packed on foundation of man-made denomination, coated with a long-lasting concealer, with blush of tradition over a made up cheek with a painted lip speaking unfruitful things, but in the eye shadow I was there, the light that gave the shadow its glooming glare

Can you hear me now? Strong the head I formed you out of the dust but somewhere down the line things went wrong turning my love into lust
Satisfying the fleshly needs of what's between your knees, a woman not found to meet your needs, your mind traces back to pornography contaminated seeds that will never be able to grow

The church, my bride should look at you and see Christ which recognizes the duties of giving security and keeping this spiritual being alive

I'm reaching out to you so grab hold of my hand, close your ears to the enemy trying to reverse my plan no need to act like a lady and think like a man this is not a movie script so pay attention to the manuscript so you can be properly equipped that your anointing may not be stripped

Can you hear me now? Step up and be what I purposely called you to be quit listening to the preaching and prophesying of false hopes and dreams trying to captivate your mind with those tangible things stop being deceived by the wolf hiding behind the sheepskin use your discernment you will know my voice when I speak. Why are you dealing with fear when I've already given you the necessary warfare tools that you need

My word, my Son, my fire and my angels which are Michael and Gabriel so if anything comes against my Kingdom it will be overthrown and outdone

Can you hear me now? I need a deeper relationship with you, communicate with me through prayer which produces passion with results that will unlock heaven on your behalf which reveals hidden agendas that bring order because out of order people can't receive my gifts many times which are things you must sacrifice to get

My word says, "blessed rather are those who hear the word of God and keep it,"

Do my will pay attention to my voice at times I may speak with correction to bring conviction but you still have been granted a choice

Can you hear me now, before I close my ear and your voice be blotted out, choose wisely because I may not speak no more

Dear God, I pray that your people will open their ears to hear you even more. Give them a greater hunger after you to even want to hear your voice. I pray that your people have a willingness to open up to you. In Jesus name I pray AMEN.

Lord, Have Your Way

So many things going on, that the pressures of life causes us to be in an uproar

No one to turn to, feeling as though in others I can't really put my trust

So I felt it was a must, I just had to do everything alone causing my life's plans to readjust

You see I once had it all, it was nothing for me to go and buy up the mall

Do me, live life because in my own eyes I was right, but overall I didn't take heed until that great fall

Everything I had gotten illegally had a spiritual recall due to me not following proper protocol

My life began to spin down a lane of destruction like a bowling ball

I was lost and confused and I needed a breakthrough

Deeply sinking using the excuse, "I'm God's work in progress," but truth is I was working on self

So here I am in a broken place

As I lift my hands as rivers of tears run down my face

I scream out of my belly, "Lord, have your way"

I surrender to you in my life at this moment make your debut, come through and cleanse my every being I beg you not to leave any residue

Crying out to God on bended knees, to me He began to speak,

"I could only get you to this place if I took you though a stripping, so as I began the rebuilding those you come in contact with will see me and know you are my offspring. Understand in this season I'm doing a new thing, no time for games because you will be penalized for mishandling your anointing in my name"

So I said, "Lord forgive me for putting my focus in those of limited resources instead of coming to you whose the ultimate, unlimited source. I open my heart, mind and spirit to receive of your outpour"

And God said, "Adhere to my instructions because this place was pre-planned, I sent word through my prophets that revival has hit the land. Just like AT&T, anybody with spiritual wifi can pick up this broadband. So be careful that you do not miss out on this clarion call because your disobedience just might have you permanently removed. My hand, my word is concrete so put it on twitter and tag me as a retweet. My Son is soon to return and I need every purpose fulfilled and complete"

So I said, "Lord, have your way in me and I praise you for the restoring. I embrace the spirit of recovery snatching back everything that the devil stole from me"

I come boldly as His mouthpiece not afraid to do ministry

As I hit these many streets declaring to the nations my God reigns above everything

I serve a God who will give you snow in the spring

Switch up the seasons and in the winter give you 80 degrees

My ears now opened to what God has to say

Your very image I want to portray flesh buried spirit submitted

So, Lord, have your way.

Dear God, have your way in the lives of your people. Lord I decree and declare that you reign and that there is no other like you. I pray that your people you give you full control in Jesus name. I thank you in advance in Jesus' name I pray AMEN.

The Plan of Salvation

Created for His purpose God made me with a plan ***(Psalms 139: 14 "I will praise thee for I am fearfully and wonderfully made: marvelous are thy works; and that my soul knoweth right well."),*** He showed His love towards me while I was yet in sin ***(Romans 5:8 "But God commandeth His love towards us in that while we were yet sinners Christ died for us.").***

Bended knees, hands lifted, ***(Philippians 2:10 "That at the name of Jesus every knee should bow of things in heaven, and things under the earth,")*** with my tongue I confess that Jesus Christ has died and risen to free me from death ***(Romans 10:9 "If thou shall confess with thy mouth the Lord Jesus and shall believe in thine heart that God hath raised him from the dead thy shall be saved.")***

His love is so rich towards me, ***(John 3:16 "For God so loved the world that He gave His only begotten son, that whosoever believeth in him shall not perish, but have everlasting life.")*** given another chance to fulfill His master plan,

So, today inducted into the Kingdom family, ***(2Corinthians 5:17 "Therefore if any man be in Christ he is a new creature, old things are passed away; behold all things are become new.")*** I am transformed with a new identity.

CONGRATULATONS!

YOU ARE SAVED!

Celebration of Freedom

I never thought that saying was true that if you play with fire you will get burned, so what I do, seems as if the things I went through the lesson was earned

You see I placed myself in a box, imprisoned by my own thoughts of constant hurt, I was seeking a way out, but being wrongfully taught only made it worse

So I hid behind a mask, but still my spirit was gripped, chains linked together of hate, anger, un-forgiveness, lying, depression, sexual perversion, and rebellion I figured I'd be like everybody else go to church and the world I'd still entertain. You see I became the new millennium renegade

Now blinded by the lust of the eyes, a real thief taking what I want because I had a good disguise in church trained to hold it together because I was told a real thug never cries

Yeah it was prophesied it's greatness in me I said, "true I'm trying to build an empire" then he said, "but you must disconnect from the world which is causing your spirit man to die," "you judging me" is what I replied

Truth be told the chains were squeezing even tighter on the inside, I was so use to going along with the crowd that it constantly kept me bound. My struggle had me paralyzed, depression had me paralyzed, unfruitful relationships had me paralyzed, and unwise counsel had me paralyzed

Stuck in a place where only He saves nothing else left but to call on His name
JESUS!!!!!!

I cry out to you with only myself to blame, so forgive me for every evil thing I've done and for straying away God spoke and said, " allow me to break these chains so that your life would never be the same I know you've gotten into this accident, but I've already paid your insurance claim

So here I stand before you FREE, eyes closed now open, the enemy a wolf in sheepskin who was really playing pretend as if he had my back, but it was a fact that my entire life was under attack my mind was twisted like a snapback now reintroduced to Christ so the world can have that

I'm so free I can't even fathom walking back through those old doors, this is not a Game Boy, PS4, Xbox or Nintendo, once a street fighter neither Mario or Luigi could save this princess no longer in bondage dipped in a new ointment I am his fresh fragrance

I'm so free, I've become a spiritual geek, my technology extends to a higher satellite carnality can't surpass receiving revelations I got more channels than Comcast I'm not a victim to my past, but victorious over that which was last

Let freedom ring from this mountain top like Dr. Martin, yes a little unorthodox, but I stand firm on Christ which is my solid rock

I'm so juiced, caffeine free, my life is no longer meaning less I shut Kool-Aid game down call me ruthless too much sweetness to him like sugar, but I'm salt preserved for a time such as this

Now untangled with what I was once entangled, I'm a part of that risen nation molded as His creation, so I declare us free a generation of ex-liars, ex-thugs, ex-divas, ex-fornicators, ex-masturbators, ex-master haters, ex-homosexuals, ex-procrastinators, ex-drug users, ex-smokers, ex-thot, ex-hypocrite, ex-idolater, ex-atheist, ex-hustler, ex-wanna be, ex-willfully sinners

Now freely righteous airs once scared, but now bear the cross on our backs with fearless confidence
One ultimate goal to build up the Kingdom of heaven so that the Kingdom of hell be destroyed lining all my ducks in a row so with this new freedom I walk in a greater season.

Dear God, I thank you for freedom and freeing your people from bondage. I pray that you give them to mindset to want to remain free. I plead the blood of Jesus over their minds and hearts. I thank you for their lives in Jesus' name I pray AMEN.

References

Poem Getting through the Wilderness of Singleness

Davis, Jessica. Getting through the Wilderness of Singleness. Lulu Publishing, 2015.

Poem Victor of the Past

Arnold "AJ Rhymez" Parks, Jr. Victor of the Past. 2013

Poem Celebration of Freedom
Canden Christina.P4CM: We are Generation Ex. online clip.Youtube.P4CM.August 7, 2009.

All poems reference the Holy Bible

About the Author

Danielle Glenn also known as Qwiet Storm is a native of Chicago, IL but currently resides in Arkansas. She is a wife and a mother first, but put a pen and a mic in her hand and she becomes Qwiet Storm an anointed poet and writer of this present age. She is a woman of God operating heavily in this arts movement including dancing and acting, to help bring forth restoration, healing, deliverance and salvation to the people of God.

To request Danielle Glenn for speaking engagements and/or send a response or testimonies about this book, please email:

qwietstormg@gmail.com

or write

Attention: Qwiet Storm

P.O. Box 5881

West Memphis, AR 72303

www.ingramcontent.com/pod-product-compliance
Lightning Source LLC
Chambersburg PA
CBHW032149040426
42449CB00005B/452